A Life Replaced

ALSO FROM POETS & TRAITORS PRESS

Advances in Embroidery by Ahmad Al-Ashqar
Relative Genitive by Val Vinokur
Education by Windows by Johnny Lorenz

A Life Replaced

Olga Livshin

poems with translations from
Anna Akhmatova & Vladimir Gandelsman

Prior publication acknowledgements appear on page 12.

Cover image and design: Alisa Rodny

Published 2019 in New York by Poets & Traitors Press
www.poets-traitors.com
poetstraitors@gmail.com

Editors: Val Vinokur, Gili Ostfield, and Julia Curl.

Published in the United States of America.

Poets & Traitors Press is an independent publisher of books of poetry and translations by a single author/translator. The press emerged from the Poet/Translator Reading Series and from the New School's Literary Translation Workshop to showcase authors who travel between writing and translation, artists for whom Language is made manifest through languages and whose own word carries, shapes, and is shaped by that of another.

Poets & Traitors Press acknowledges support from Eugene Lang College, the New School Bachelor's Program for Adults and Transfer Students, and the New School Foreign Languages Department.

ISBN: 978-0-9990737-3-5

For my mother
and in memory of my father

A Life Replaced

CONTENTS

FOREWORD

Haunted by exile, longing for linkages between past and present, Olga Livshin's A Life Replaced is a collection of poetry that wants to spread a "blanket of wild buckwheat / over a meadow"—and does just that. What is the meadow of this book? It is memory, both personal and collective, bringing voices of many poets, spoken through the same mouth to us in English: "it is summer everywhere, except war."

This is a book where childhood comes alive, and we see Livshin's parents and various other citizens in a city known for its laughter. There is the legendary Odessa poet Yuri Mikhailik "wrestling with phlox" in the "Soviet Socialist Republic of Tomato Plants."

And then the page of life is torn from a book: we see immigrants, refugees, pain. What salves this pain? What glues the pages back into books? The love of poets is the connective tissue. Livshin is in conversation with two poetic masters, our contemporary Vladimir Gandelsman, and a great 20th-century poet Anna Akhmatova.

Gandelsman is a much-respected Russian-Jewish poet in exile, a poet of great music and no illusions. "Go ahead, open the door," he says, "lean your heart against the wall." Gandelsman knows life in exile, in a "strange American town / with a mysterious capacious name." He knows that even isolation can be a gift for a lyric poet. In exile, he says, "I flinched and recognized myself." What saves him? Love, even in the form of elegy. His elegy for his mother is one of the best in Russian in the last few decades.

And then there is the great poetic mother, Anna Akhmatova. A grand poet who is a guiding spirit for many of us, in any language. Livshin's Akhmatova is both the wise poet and a character in Livshin's own poems. Even in the United States, under President Winter, in a fugue of Russian-American depressive episodes, the echo of Akhmatova's formal music and gracious tone is clear: "Here comes my verse, already brazen, tender / for you, for me, for joy."

This is a book that lays all its cards on the table. We see poetic influences, yes. We see conversations, yes. We see various voices as they enter Livshin's life. But we also see the music of play, both textual and mundane, play that allows others to enter and tango and transform. This a strange book—hauntingly beautiful and unforgettable.

— Ilya Kaminsky, author of *Deaf Republic*

ACKNOWLEDGMENTS

A warm cup of Odessa mint tea to the editors of the publications where some of these poems and translations have appeared: *Kenyon Review Online* ("Annas at the Stove"), *Breakwater Review* ("Thoreau in Russia"), *Mad Hatters' Review* ("Mom Is Scared" and Vladimir Gandelsman's "Untitled [A bird builds up to a whole...]," and "A child is sleeping..."), *Jacket* ("Russian 101" and "Dressing a Memory"), *Off the Coast* ("Martial Arts"), *Writers Resist* ("Something There Is That Doesn't Love"), *International Poetry Review* ("To Russia, With You"), *The Matador Review* ("Eating a Persimmon, 1954"), *Gyroscope Review* ("Milk Mushrooms"), *Eleven Eleven* (Gandelsman's "The snow must fly..."), *Construction* ("Akhmatova for Our Times"), *Rise Up Review* ("Translating a Life"), *The Common* (Gandelsman's "Immigrant Ditty"), *The Massachusetts Review* (Gandelsman's "I walked by a school..."), and *Transom* (Anna Akhmatova's "Memory's Voice," "Untitled [A grieving prophetess, you've dropped your hands...]," and "O.S. [from *Poem Without a Hero*]." The latter three translations were also reprinted by *Poetry International*.

Thank you to Dawn Hogue and Lisa Vihos for including "Translating a Life" in *From Everywhere a Little: A Migration Anthology*.

Thank you to Paulann Petersen for selecting "To Russia, With You" as a runner-up to the 2016 Lois Cranston Memorial Prize from CALYX.

So much gratitude to the Virginia Center for the Creative Arts and the Writers' Colony at Dairy Hollow for their sustenance.

Deepest affection to my mentors, Janet Sylvester and Rosanna Warren.

Thank you to Maggie Smith for her comments on an earlier version of this book, and to Ellen Goldstein for her meticulous and inspired copyediting.

Thank you to Lynn Siegel, Linda González, Linda Geraghty, and Noelle Hammerbacher for their professional, compassionate support.

Thank you to my family, friends, and community of writers. I am grateful to everyone who gave me feedback on the poems and translations: Alexander Burry, Julia Kolchinsky Dasbach, Tom Dolack, Kerstin Fuchs, Maria Gapotchenko, Olena Jennings, Harriet Levin Millan, Janet Sylvester, Kathleen Witkowska Tarr, and Nina Wieda.

Love to Andrew Janco, my partner in translation crime. Hugs and puns to Nathan Janco, comrade in silliness.

Thank you to Poets & Traitors Press for giving this project a home, with rooms for both poems and translations.

Lifelong gratitude to my mother and father, for everything. This book is for them.

IN COLD WE TRUST
(A WORD FROM THE AUTHOR)

I came to the United States with my parents during what seemed to be the aftermath of the only cold war, and what turned out to be only an interlude. It is clear, in 2019, that we are living during a new, more inventive cold war—and in a quiet, episodic civil war.

This book is an attempt to see the United States. as a complex country, a place of compassion and tribalism and social justice and intense hatred. And hope, for specific people with their specific actions.

The particulars are important. We landed in San Diego, a troubled, culturally rich city on the border. My junior high school was severely internally segregated, with knife fights between different groups and phoned-in bomb threats. A month after we arrived, two kids attacked me as I walked to gym class, because I was the wrong kind and in the wrong place. I still have a scar, a little icy tattoo. I also have a memory of what happened after: the PE teacher insisted on driving me home, rather than let me get on the bus. When she stopped for gas, she asked if she could get me something—a soda? an ice cream? What happened earlier, she said, was *not what this country was like.* I was shocked, after all our Russian cynicism, and could not decide what was more surprising: the attack or my teacher's genuinely patriotic statement. "Balloons!" my teacher determined, standing with me at the gas station counter. "I am going to—buy you balloons!"

Millions of perfect strangers—perfectly wonderful strangers—welcome us, and each other. And yet there is, was, and may always be another America, the one with its own historical wounds as well as xenophobic aspirations—and, lately, outcries and crimes. These days, when even naturalized citizens of the United States are being denaturalized, my American life can be revoked at any time. The America this book attempts to describe is not hateful; neither do I picture it as Janus-faced. It includes immigrants and our own oversized emotional baggage. And the gyrations of nativist fear. And the possibility of this country as a refuge, only enabled by individuals, never by governments as a whole.

I also wanted to explore the complexity of what certain versions of my native culture might mean, aside from the statements made by the current Russian thug-in-charge. I do not mean to suggest that it is possible to forget the Russia that intervenes in other countries' elections and marches into other countries under the slogan of pan-Slavism. I do not wish to push it all aside and start celebrating Russian tea and cookies and—dare I say—ballet?

What I mean is that there are the other Russians: Anna Akhmatova, and our contemporary, the poet Vladimir Gandelsman, among them. Translating these poets allows me to reach for something from my own Russian past and to add others' Russian childhood experiences to my own. This book includes selections from their work and my poems written in dialogue with Akhmatova and Gandelsman.

The poems I selected for this collection speak to me at this time of hatred, in our country. Akhmatova (1889–1966) provides inspiration for moral strength at times of terror: this, after all, is what *Requiem*, her tale of sorrow and survival in Stalin's time is known for in the West. Less obviously, Akhmatova is also painstakingly honest in facing her own vulnerability and desperation at such periods in history. The intensity with which she admits her fear and her defeat amaze me. Rather than paint our own attempts at resistance as heroic, Akhmatova can teach us a kind of lucid humility.

Gandelsman is very much the literary child of the poets of the Russian Silver Age such as Akhmatova: he draws on their dramatic, spiritually intense version of modernism. Born in 1948, he is another poet from St. Petersburg (born in what was, then, post-war Leningrad). For many years, Gandelsman wrote in the oblivion of the literary underground; after coming to the United States in 1991, he was first able to publish his work, and is now highly acclaimed in Russia, where he won the Moscow Reckoning Prize, the highest award for poetry. He now divides his time between New York and St. Petersburg.

Both Akhmatova and Gandelsman are ecstatic voices. As a young poet, Akhmatova was part of the Acmeist school, poets who went to the *acme*, the highest point of expression, whether meditating on fleeting moments or on major historical events. Gandelsman is a post-Acmeist poet, and he, too, brings an amazing clarity to moments of both delight and sorrow. His exquisite diction and surprising collages of words help us remember our own moments of heightened feeling.

I especially admire Gandelsman's poetry that explores the thorny aspects of early years in immigration. It is with candor and acmeistically expressive detail that he treats the slow dying of the self that happens to many middle-aged immigrants in the United States—a topic Akhmatova would never need to touch, since she stayed in Soviet Russia through its many torturous decades. Gandelsman was forty-two when he came to the U.S., the same age as my mother when she arrived. For an adult steeped in his original culture—and a representative of that culture—it can be extremely hard to adapt. Gandelsman's speaker cannot identify with the American cultural landscape. What he does, instead, is map a world of immigrant push-and-pull—of alienation and attraction to the new home. It is there that darkly comical Russian-English mixtures ("beeldeeng," "feefty-feefty") belie the integrity of the speaker's lofty poetic diction. It is there, too, that the speaker experiences a spiritual connection with a small American boy.

I feel as though Gandelsman gives me permission to speak honestly about people and places beyond those delimited by the mini-utopia of the American dream. A thankful voice, he also enables me to speak of awe: for community, and family, and my adopted country's capacity for social justice. Gandelsman's gratitudes are, of course, different: he is thankful for birds, and paintings, and the memory of a parent, her neuroses and all.

Both Gandelsman and Akhmatova cherish the wild authenticity of childhood and adolescence. They see those years as a rich source of the sensual feeling of life-as-is. Akhmatova called childhood an "important and profound period," the time when one sees and feels clearly. In her poems written in Stalin's time, she repeatedly evokes her teenage years, trying to give them—and herself—another life. Feverishly, tenderly, she recalls her youth, the brazenness of her café nights and love triangles, and her very likely romantic fascination with the actress-dancer-puppeteer Olga Glebova-Sudeikina. The remembrance of her youth's daring keeps Akhmatova from being suffocated by her time.

Gandelsman is a terrific champion of childhood. In one of his poems, a bakery glowing on the corner becomes a quasi-religious experience for a boy who craves "pastry delicacies" and adores the "pink maidens" who sell them. The bakery is a spiritually charged—and recharging—memory for the now-grown boy, decades later.

As for my approach to translating these poets, I find inspiration in Gandelsman's statement in one of the poems included here: that art is made "out of one soul, then / out of another." Even if the translation of a poem replaces the original, posturing as the real deal—like many of us immigrants, seeking to be authentically local but never quite fitting the bill—translation is also an augmentation of creative energies. An energizing clarity animates a work in one language and self; when another artist participates, their vision is added to it. If life is constant loss, they, together, make a doubly rich phenomenon, reality's lush double fire.

Andrew Janco helped me with most of the translations included here. My love, who enables me to translate those I love, Andrew is another layer of the journey "out of one soul, then / another." I am especially awed by working with an American trained in Russian history, who is willing to delve into the troubled waters of my native culture and to see what survives of our various shipwrecks. He is willing, later, to sit on the shore with me and meditate on their meanings. Then we create our highly subjective English versions, and display them to the world. In this war, all of his involvement is especially precious.

I know our distortions of the originals too well and make no claims that this is the True Akhmatova or the Definitive Edition of Gandelsman. But they caused a spark, and our mutual bonfire is helping me survive this particular winter.

WHERE IT USED TO BE HOME

~

With Anna Akhmatova

TRANSLATING A LIFE

for O.M. and M.R.

Someone spread a blanket of wild buckwheat
over a meadow. Someone tucked puffball pillows
in each corner of the purple-green sheet.
It is summer everywhere, except war.
War, where it used to be home,
and now, war by government, here.
And what does it matter that the meadow
seduces the bees in pollen, or me in lines
of a poem, or that I hear perfectly good
Russian names for plants and translate them
into You-and-Me-ish? Take the tea mushroom,
the little fox mushrooms and piggies,
the early field-dweller, the mysterious
cheese-eater. These words are undocumented
here, and the country that sent them erases
every syllable with its crimes.
Take an under-birch-mushroom
anyway—it's a choice edible,
birch bolete in your tongue, on
the tongue. The language for falling in love
with forests, and stories, and friends
does not care who's killing whom.
Unfortunately, I care. And, sitting here
by a huge flowering bush, I see no refuge.
What languaged fantasy could stop us
from being murderous strangers? Would you
take a Russian mushroom name,
tuck it in your lapel for the brief banquet of life?
Does that translate anything else for you? Is this
how it works?

CALL IT LONGING

After Joy Harjo

There is this edge, where some of us recall childhood's voices.—There is an edge, Mama i Papa—where we wake up in the car with a travel mug to recall a Country.—No, not that Country of the Present slowly invading this one.—

There is a threshold inside me, as I watch the ceramic-metallic molecule of the highway grow and explode and go past.—But what I see is the alley of Grandpa's apricot trees, their branches growing backwards into the earth.—

That's how That Country functions, my beloved liberal radio will say.—*Ambition to dominate the world.*—The radio will be right, with its comforting, frightening, heated fresh air. —*No matter the cost.*—

There is an edge—*Peter the Great, Ivan the Terrible, Putin the Nauseating,* says the radio—where people like us, for some reason, also exist.

To drive—

To the Soviet Socialist Republic of Tomato Plants scratching at my feet—to your friend Mikhailik wrestling with phlox to get to our dinner table and read us his latest poems—to the Principalities of Mama's Hip Pianist Friends who improvised jazz—

To the Sovereign State of Leave Me Alone!—with the juniper twins, the raspberries, and the doves—

And to the Backwards Nation of Empty Heaven—filling up
at fourteen when we immigrated—pushing myself out—love,
then illness—our small son feeding both parakeets at the
same time—peace—this American life—

Which is where I land.—In traffic, at the top of the hour,
listening about the Other Country's desire to destroy us.—
To drive.—Like the other NPRicans, fast and catlike in our
super-special talking cars—greatly-bothered-slash-supremely-
helpless.—*Join us tomorrow night as we discuss Another Country of
Nuclear Weapons.*

There is this irresistible edge of the highway, where I pull
over and call you.

Allo?—I remember you two covered the currant bushes for
the winter, you spread the tablecloth printed with yellow
chicks on the table.—Patiently you grew worlds out of a
country.—You know how to be as soft and dreamlike as
apricots, and I am from you, first and last. No one can hurt
me now.

A.A.

***

What makes this century worse than any before it?
Maybe that, for once, it noticed the world's sorrows,
black smoke rising from them. And it touched the heart
of this most painful ulcer. Still, it could not heal this.

The earthly sun's still shining in the west;
our cities' roofs, still blazing in its rays...
Here a white creature chalks the houses of the dead
with crosses, calls the ravens, and the ravens fly.

NEWSCAST AKHMATOVA

Always the same question. *What makes this century worse than any before it?*—the twenty-year-old Anna asks in a poem.

Her century swelled with the inequities of all the previous ones.—I grew up there—at the end of the revolution that overflowed by seventy years—was rocked with the tight-lipped grief of her poems—quoted by my mother, who had her face—whose face I now wear.

What news for her would make an adequate reply?

*

News: I have now lived most of my life in a country that, as Akhmatova would say, is *relatively vegetarian.*—People aren't the main staple of its diet.—Immigrants the world over say, *We didn't come to this country, that country, or that country—any country* but—*to mourn our lives.*

But the country where I went to high school, college, and grad school, where I later taught at my alma mater—*school* is one of the favorite dishes.—Routine cannibalism.—Bomb threats: we were evacuated into the parking-lot sunshine.— Spit three times over the shoulder: you and you, but not you, will avoid being eaten.

*

News: After three days in labor, I saw my son. Warmth rushed through me as I lay cut up, belly up.—I said: *We'll have so much fun together, you and I.*

The word *fun* thus entered my overcast Russian worldview.—
Every day I meet him after school: he colors the world
cerulean.

*

Anna Andreyevna's son spent most of his life in a prison
camp.—Because of his origins.—She could not rescue him
even by writing odes to Stalin.—Most readers do not know,
or else cannot remember, whether she wrote such odes.—She
did.

*

Old news: Russia is carnivorous.—New news: now carnivorous
beyond its borders.

Sort-of-new news: this country never stopped being
carnivorous.—America's eye, more technologically avian,
looks into every home.—News: we might need a different
word than *home*.

*

In the home of her poetry, Akhmatova has found room
for her whole country.—Found a chronology: from lush
turn-of-the-century eroticism to imprisonment—to oblivion,
intended—but not accomplished—by the state.—In her stance
of the memory keeper, she stood immovable.—Like a steppe
baba statue: Paleolithic, gray; huge.

*

At the end of her life, Akhmatova said: *My life had been
replaced.*

*

News: A few years back, a young woman in Moscow founded
the first hospice for children in Russia.—This woman, a
friend of mine, is now in her early thirties, a seasoned
administrator for the hospice, somewhat cynical.—Her
hospice, that colorful refuge, is still alive.—

*

Because my replies are like light touch, their comfort cool
and faithless, each fingertip a raindrop.—I refuse to be
separated from her: to sum her up.—She is needed.

*

Who, me? you ask. You seem amused.

Your rhetorical questions are needed, for they demand
a specific integrity from each of us.—Your stone house of
womanhood is needed, a house of protest.

You are the one with the news for this next century: *This
century is worse than those before it. Change something.*

A NIGHT IN THE HISTORY OF THE COLD

for N.T.

SUBURBIA, USA — A wool coat rides with me in my car.
Tall and stately, it luxuriates in the back seat

atop two trash bags stuffed with winter clothes.
The day after Donald Trump was elected president,

my new friend gave me the coat for the refugees
who had come to our city that fall,

for the tenderness that stood small
in the icy park where we met. We chatted in Russian,

which we yearned to claim as our own.
My five-year-old ran around with Nina's boy,

brandishing charred marshmallows.
This moment is brought to you by President-Elect Winter—

shivers, cold you very much, President-Elect.
May I introduce you to Interim President Warmth,

Specialist in Jerry-Rigging Words Such As "Refuge"
Until We Have Something Better? What's that? Not

cool enough? Well. Soon I'll pass him, hug-to-hug,
into Charlotte's arms, the arms of another stranger who ran

towards me thanks to you, Mr. Refrigerated Aisle.
In two days, Charlotte amassed a trailer of tiny jackets

and XL cotton sweaters from people who tried to do—
something–after you were anointed. After I hand over

the clothes, what choice will be left for us?
But right now, there is something softer

than fear. It is in my car. I have touched it.

A.A.

***

I have no need for odes—their wordy battles—
Or elegies, those dainty parlor games.
To me, in poetry, everything should be out of line,
Not how these things are done.

I wish you knew what garbage sprouts poems
And grows them without an ounce of shame,
Like yellow dandelions rising by a fence,
Like burdocks, weeds.

An angry, "Stop!", the smell of just-spilled tar,
Some mystery mold spreading on the wall—
Here comes my verse, already brazen, tender,
For you, for me, for joy.

AKHMATOVA FOR OUR TIMES

Pasting Akhmatova into Google Translate,
and clicking "ENGLISH," one sees a plausible
quatrain, if somewhat misunderstood:

"Wherefrom what litter poetry grows
Shame knowing not:
Like a yellow dandelion by the fence,
Like mugs and quinoa."

The poor neural network mistook violet burdocks
for mugs. Less mysteriously, purslane metastasized
into quinoa. Shame remained goddamn fucking shame.

This Akhmatovaish is a recipe, its ingredients staples
available in every home today: mugs, quinoa, shame.
Combine, cry, and bake in your phone. You and I

already burn in it, homunculi rage-crisped from the latest
assault on our sisters and brothers, the statements of their
skin, or accent, or sex. You will get

no dandelions at the end—a few more gobs of shame.
Perhaps it's not a recipe, and means just that
you can plant quinoa in a mug. Google it: you can

make it grow. Use unwashed, unpolished seeds.

PRELUDE

Every morning, online, it snows fresh missives
by my beloveds on the other cheek of the globe.
One love sits on a beach, wishing Crimea
were Goa. Our mutual country ate this peninsula
with its palaces, palm trees. She plans not to tell
her daughter, not yet: the little one, who digs,
using her plastic Russian princesses as shovels,
all the way to Turkey, probably—here's the selfie.
Her Royal Highness Masha has too much sand
in her hair. Social media make me a goddess
watching benevolently over friends, liking or loving
them with genuine guilt. Another beloved wanders
in the divine snowflakes of St. Petersburg, sees
cops, trucks, Port-a-Potties, and asks: *What's this
commotion?* A blushing youth explains: *Lady,
that would be the Festival of Youth for Peace,
Solidarity, and the Struggle against Imperialism.*
My friend exclaims: *What, again??*
Again: What? could be the title for a Russian
culture class, and I could be its prophet,
but this will not stop the snow from falling.
Look: a tattooed love, a freezing room,
we are not here nor queer, we are invisible,
but her girlfriend says, *You are tortik, moi
tortik,* my cakey, by way of proposing;
and probably slaps her beloved, just guessing,
on her beautiful ass. Why else post these
engaged faces on Instagram? Laughing,
laughing, as if the law were on their side,
and we all lived in Onlineland. I am one
unhelpful voyeur. My six-year-old comes in,
turns off my laptop, demands that I read:

Cheburashka was a damaged toy with huge ears,
then he was shipped in a crate of oranges
to a wonderful place, where he found his best friend,
Crocodile Ghena. I read in Russian, my son asks
in English: *Why did the crocodile want to help*
the children? Who gave Cheburashka the bricks
to build the House of Peace, Solidarity, and
the Struggle against Imperialism? Why
did you leave that wonderful place? A second
falls out of time like an eyelash.
For that second, I am made out of my child,
and someone turns off the snow.

FUGUE

When a Russian-American walks away from her American home
    into a depressive episode—into a Nor'easter—

When she stops by a church and American God is out to lunch—
    outside colorless chips swish—indifferent God is
    brushing his teeth—

When the world is shifting and rearranging itself   When the word
    home runs away from under her feet—tiny globe—
    little ball—rabbit

When this American-Russian no longer knows where she is
    when she hears one car in the desperate quiet and
    rushes to be hit—

When
      she stops at the curb

And trudges instead towards a café and sits down shaking in
her hoodie—
    Russian—and her tea, scalding, American—

And her husband texts her *Come home* and she types *Where's that*
    and he texts her *With me*—

When she texts him *Come get me*
    She is temporarily made of love

A.A.

NORTHERN ELEGIES: FIVE

> Blessed be the man who visited this world
> During one of its fate-changing moments.
> —Tyutchev[1]

Like a river,
I was deflected by this bitter era.
My life had been replaced. It ran
inside another riverbed, or past another,
and I know nothing of these banks—my own.
The spectacles that I was forced to miss:
o, how the curtain rose without me, fell
the same way. All the friends—my own—
I never met. The contours of the cities
that could have made me cry. I saw none,
I know one city in the whole world,
and I can even find it in my sleep.

So many poems I could have written,
their secret chorus wandering around me;
someday it might just smother me...
I've known the beginnings and the ends,
and life after the end, and something
that one should not recall these days.
Some other woman took my one and only place,
my name—the only legal name I had—
and left my funny moniker to me,
that I used up for all it could lend me.
I won't lie down into my own grave, alas.
Yet sometimes, suddenly, the reckless wind of spring,
a passage in a book I came across,

1 Fyodor Ivanovich Tyutchev (1803-1873) was a Russian poet and
diplomat.

a stranger's smile—any of this pulls me back
into a lifetime that did not take place.
In such-and-such year, that event would happen,
in that year, plans: to travel, watch, and think,
remembering; to enter a new love,
like entering a mirror, with the dull realization
that infidelity happens, and that wrinkle,
which was not there just yesterday...

....

Yet if I looked from there upon my present life,
I could—at last—find out how envy feels...

1945, Leningrad

KIDNAPPED AKHMATOVA

Anna-Anna, swaddled in your hosanna-inducing scarf, with its long tassels of sorrow, wake up. Let me take you—*the spectacles I was forced to miss*—you wrote futile letters begging for your friends to be released from labor camps—*o, how the curtain rose without me, fell the same way*—let me take you—now that you are asleep and weightless.

We'll go to the tender tawdry Russia of the end of the twentieth century.—When all windows flew open.—I think you'll like the show.

I am seven, all scraped knees and elbows. Anna-Bo-Banna-Banna-Fo-Fanna-Fanna-et-cetera, let's have you be—the same age as me. Look, right by my house! Big, tall women wearing woven wristbands with multihued threads!—They gave me one!—They are called *hippies*!—Guitars strummed in the ancient lane called Crooked Knee.—Guitars, leaned against the ancient church that still functions as a warehouse for potatoes.—Anna, will you bend your knees in black chiffon, will you sit with us in the glorious dust, will you take a break from history?

Look, Anna-Bella: Russia is as whimsical as us. We both love swimming in the Black Sea. In the 1900s they scold you: swimming is uncouth for a maiden. In the 1990s I have an uncle-as-outpost in America: check out my amazing leopard print bikini. Would you want this cheap paradise, Anna?

Let's fly past the sea, into the mountains.—The tiny airplane is full of human sparrows who chirp at us in a language I've never heard, but I bet you have: *They're French*, my mother hisses me down the aisle, *stop staring*.—I am wearing a turquoise, embroidered dress, the hard-to-find Chinese

Dress. Do *you* think it's the best dress ever, Ann?—One birdie, smelling like a perfume shop, grabs at the hem of my dress, tweets about it with her friend.—Am I real, Anna?

Poetry in the 90s, you ask? Everywhere.—Everything that was sensical flew open, became a peacock.—Let's go to the Arbat; look at the man on a streetlamp reciting his poetry, look at the people afraid to be arrested for unsanctioned listening.— Take a rest, Anna.

Anna of terse love poems, I am twelve and fallen in crush.— With my American, gorgeous, pudgy teacher Jon, walking up the hills of bloody, cracked Moscow, its car exhaust flecking his Doc Martens.—Sit with me outside the school, Anya: do you think he has read my love note?—It's three hours after school.—You are I are still girls; like you, I have no right to what is most important.—There is no break, Anna.

Before I was pried away from that country by my well-meaning parents, before that country regained its appetite for blood, it had this moment: the underground Club Poetry read a novel out loud, on a commuter train, about a commuter train.—The 1968 novel about a commuter train full of alcoholics.—A patchwork of Proletarianese, and Exquisite Poetese by the likes of you, Anna Andreyevna.—You fragrant person, making other people's lives impossible.—They yearned for a past they wanted to recover.—Did you live, Anna?

The poets read that novel on the train where it was written.— That train, carrying drunks and memory: to Eden?—Was that your train? Where did you go?

A.A.

MEMORY'S VOICE

For O.A. Glebova-Sudeikina

What is it that you see on the wall,
with a dull gaze, in the light of late dawn?

A seagull on the blue tablecloth of the sea
or Florentine blossoming trees?

Or the place where worry crossed your path,
in Tsarskoye Selo, in the enormous park?

Is it he, who once lay beside you,
and chose a white death over your prison?

No, I see only the wall—and on it, some last gleams,
the fading of celestial flames.

June 18, 1913, Slepnyovo

MARTIAL ARTS

The night Sandy Hook's children were killed,
I bought four boxes of pancake mix. Kolya's
mom, that's me. I wanted an underground
bullet-proof bunker. Whole Foods had to do.

Eight p.m. I walked across the glittering street.
My kindergartner shouted: Mama, my Mama,
let's have thousands of breakfasts and live
an awesome American life! A black belt

in breakfast, that's what I want, punching life
with pan-fried suns every morning.
I'd wrap my son in silky camouflage
of flapjacks and hotcakes, those warm secrets

that English opens for the newly arrived.
But Kolya peeks out from history: Mama, my
Mama, what do you do all day long but think of the kids
who were almost me, who put on little rain boots

on a real morning before someone swept away
all their trains and dinosaurs, dolls and small clowns,
and so many packages, all sorts of presents,
tons of purchases pinning us to the ground?

A.A.

***

To Olga Glebova-Sudeikina

A grieving prophetess, you've dropped your hands,
your locks sticking to your ashen forehead.
Oh, that red, delicious smile seduced
so many queen bees, stained
the cheeks of many butterflies.

Your eyes are clear, far-gazing, moonlike,
transfixed. What's this expression: tender
remorse for him, who died? Or gracious
forgiveness to the living
for your exhaustion, for your long disgrace?

1921

DRESSING A MEMORY

> Моя радость [mo YAH RAH dost]:
> sweetheart; literally, "my joy" (Russian)

I can't picture you, sometime lover.
You fold into memory with such skill and grace
that I suspect it is what takes place

between grownups. Well, these are child words:
Моя радость, a lantern on some other life,
I still feel your sudden warmth.

I still hear the sigh of language
from the tiny seed that you planted.
I want you in ridiculous Russian,

I want you, dressed only in that little expression,
which you made so sparklingly literal,
and which is just soundsplash to you.

Moh; yah; rah: these are grunts or wailings—
like the sounds of what your desire was.
We are even: we made for each other

this language, without translation.

A.A.

FROM POEM WITHOUT A HERO

Second Dedication
To O.S.

Is it you, Little Farce, you, Psyche,[2]
    your black-and-white fan
        wafting over me? Do you want to
share a secret—that you already
    traveled over the Lethe,
        now breathe in a different
kind of spring? Don't dictate words,
    I hear them: a warm rain presses
        on the roof; in the ivy, whispers.
A tiny being was planning to live,
    she sprouted, puffed out, wanted
        to shine in a new jacket.
I am sleeping—
        she alone above me—
    she, whom people call Spring, she—
        I named her Loneliness.
I am sleeping—
        our youth in my dreams,
    and that cup, which passed from HIM.
        When I wake up,
I can give it to you
as a keepsake,
    like a clean flame in the clay
        or a daffodil in an open grave.

May 25, 1945
The Fountain House[3]

2 "Little Farce, Psyche": the heroine of the eponymous play by Yuri Belyayev. [Translator's note: *Psyche* and *Little Farce, or The Year 1840* were two plays by Belyaev. Glebova-Sudeikina played the heroine in each, at the Maly Theater of the Literary and Artistic Club led by Alexey Suvorin.]

3 [Translator's note: the Fountain House (Фонтанный Дом), the mansion in St. Petersburg also known as the Sheremetevsky Palace before the Russian Revolution, was Akhmatova's home from 1925 to 1952. She lived in a small room inside an apartment that belonged to the mansion.]

ANNAS AT THE STOVE

> Manuscripts do not burn.
> —Mikhail Bulgakov, *The Master and Margarita*

Akhmatova stands
by the wood stove
with Anna Ahrens
in the kitchen of the apartment they shared,
on the morning after the man they shared
was arrested.

They all lived together,
the compromise,
forced on them—
until eleven last night.
Now that Nikolasha is gone, all that matters
burns—anything compromising.

Anna asks Anna: "But what is
compromising?"
Men are siphoned like random bits of cream
from fermenting modern families.
Women behave as ordered,
cook with ash.

Into the fire,
Nikolai Punin's work:
Apollon. Other posh
literary journals.
His articles about Futurists.
Art history.

Ahrens whispers: "Anything could be
evidence. What's on his desk?"
A doctor, a good cook,
she knows how to solve problems,
how to approach immolation
as a task.

The poetess clutches the doctor's hand:
"What will happen to Nikolasha
if we erase his past? If he doesn't return,
if he can't fill it in, will you
help me remember?"
"*But he's coming back!*" Ahrens

shouts. "He's coming back!"
"Hush," the mistress says
to the wife, embraces her
by the faint embers, whispering
to hush her own doubt: "We
will bring it all back."

IN A STRANGE AMERICAN TOWN

~

With Vladimir Gandelsman

V.G.

IMMIGRANT DITTY

The sun goes down. The supermarket
floods with dead light. Now the gate
caws at you in the near darkness.
A not-so-magic key might blaze.

Can't steal happiness, now, can you?
Win Lotto America! Now, this,
as they call it, is a *beeldeeng*,
this is *garrbage*; nothing—this.

Go ahead, open the door.
Lean your heart against the wall.
The world doesn't need you anymore,
bottom-swimming little fish.

Fruit are morphing into veggies.
It's the middle of the fall.
Someone, please, come to my rescue,
let me breathe a little here.

Eenie, meanie, minie, moe,
there goes a very average schmo.
It's to sleep he waddles off
on his short, well-trodden path.

Is that some Carmen being stabbed
at this late hour I hear?
Or the howl of the parked pooches
sniffing out their little thieves?

It's an envelope, its torn edge.
The edge of a land not settled by you.
It's the echoes of dumb music
brought to you by Puerto Ricans.

Poet, sleep! It's you who's awful.
Sing your fears some bedtime songs.
Lull your fear of *balldeeng* autumn,
darkly bronzed in the Bronx woods.

It's the *feefty-feefty* birdie
tweeting all alone at dawn.
It's the elevator-riding,
lifeless yellow afternoon.

Demons swirl the rags of plastic
bags around the street all day.
Life is finite; death, undying;
a brain, trembling; this, its air.

THE FACE OF EXILE

For L.N.

LATTAKIA, SYRIA–PHILADELPHIA, USA–

see: flight—shelter—nostalgia, in that order.
The signature look of exile, that patina-coated profile,
ennobled by Ovid, suspiciously granted
to people born where you were. Someone
banished you; he will be punished, and soon.
For now, we exiles' great-grandkids let you in,

but why is the face so gay, delicate, yours?
Puffs of ginger fur float around your face.
Your mouth is filled with *kasha varnishkes*
of words—one language, under God, indivisible—
undercooked, while two others taste of kibbeh
and cherries, no matter how much

you try to forget. What if you care most
about your sister's wedding, which you missed,
not having seen your family in years? That's not
nostalgia. And this isn't a face. The ass-crack
of exile, the beak of flight, light turned around
by running webbed feet. Sir, ma'am—dammit,

person—you are supposed to stop running.
You have arrived in exile... Enough. If we stop
calling you our words, we may yet see you
as ambiguous as our own families. See that your
story is to be continued, distilled, for now,
as wild sadness in your lips,
which shape your own mangled truth:

My sister is named Nareman.
See the picture on my phone? See how she presides
over the family in her tiara? See her white dress,
that fountain of light? Spills into every corner
of all you can see from here.

V.G.

***

A child is sleeping, one hand under
her cheek, the other
hugging a doll. She is not dreaming of guilt;
she is profoundly right.

Like a deep layer of snow
asleep in an empty yard:
no factories nearby, no
dark figures knee-deep in mud.

The snow in the empty yard
is like the child asleep:
consisting, radiantly,
only of itself.

V.G.

***

I walked by a school in a strange American town
with a mysterious, capacious name.
(I lived there then). Not far, Spring stood,
holding some piquant flower
in her gradually tender hand.

School had just ended, and the sun
cast wide its fishing net, and caught
a pale child walking down the steps,
squinting his eyes to nearly-shut.

Mothers looked on as a son or daughter
came out of the doors, leaving their horror
behind, where a child multiplies the $sin(x)$
by the utter minus of their knowledge.
Let's go, where the sky shines, blueing,
and a stripe in the sky melts, widening,
running after a great big jet plane!

I walked and listened to Spring's notes.
The clock struck two. A double fire
lit up the square. A timer started
to tick, promising an explosion;
it smelled a lot like school vacation;
the child ran, picking at a petal,
ahead, towards his mom and me.
I flinched and recognized myself.

What had just happened wasn't
a memory. That is the point.

My friend, o April's magic hat tricks,
that time of mystic substitutions!
Ol' Marcie Proust, ol' Georgie Borges
described this phenomenon in their works.
Perhaps Nabokov took some stabs
at something like this. We'll affix
our philosophical bit to theirs.

Do not regret this short life: you are
inches away from immortality
when, one spring day, you find yourself
behind the lining of your jacket.
Oh, people! In our gloomy days,
they need a flick on their old noses
to believe in anything. You
are simultaneous to yourself—
remember! And God be with you.

And here's the last point: only moments
after you're drawn into the world,
you are already making sad the dot
where you once were—and now you're not.
You become duller, like a fish
dimming with sorrow in the sand.

Immortal friend, my friend, don't grieve.
Carry yourself back into the void.

I came to a river, I couldn't remember
where I had come from, why I came,
or where I was going. Fishing nets
lay empty by my feet, and, God,
my heart was light—was finally light.

June 1997

EATING A PERSIMMON, 1954

At four years old, in her grandpa's lap,
sun-warmed inside an Odessa courtyard,
my mother tests out a persimmon.

She has never met such weird fruit:
sweet jellyfish creepy-crawling.
Nu, es, little *meydeleh,* eat,

her grandpa glows at her, a Jewish wizard
visiting from a collective farm.
His beard smells like cow poop.

In quiet Russian, she asks: *Grandpa,*
do people actually like per-sim-mons?
Oh, *mansy!* Silly stories!—he brushes her off.—

Is this why I walked all over the Privoz Market
for one perfect piece of fruit I could afford—
just for you? Have some good selch and eat.

My mother sighs and tries to swallow the globe,
which spins sixty quick times around the sun,
finding her with her grandson and me,

all of us considering a bowl of conical,
identical supermarket Hachiyas, freckled
by California, where she lives these days.

And this story she tells us. And Adam,
with his *nyet, thanks but no thanks, Grandma,*
for that fruit. And my mom, who decides

to reveal, then, the DNA of our family's
eating: a pogrom, she says, chewed up
her uncle, a violinist, as he ran to shelter;

the world chomped on a branch
of our family like a deer, just needing to eat,
just minding its own business,

for instance, a six-year-old boy—
had he not died, he'd be an older brother
to my mother. She was not born yet,

the first child to sprout in that great
mishpooha after the war. *They all gave me treats,*
she smiles sadly. *Going a bit hungry themselves.*

I ask what a treat was back then. *A handful
of sugar?* How godlike, that persimmon,
I think to myself. My mother's grandpa

must have imagined he gave her the chance
to be—just this once—the eater.
How, instead, he gave her

an order, force-feeding the love of forced
feeding, the unsubtle art of forcing
that I spoon-feed to Adam, with a dash

of Russian, which passes for some
Vitamin R—to make a child Feel Rooted.
How there may still be a persimmon

here: couldn't my great-grandfather
want his only grandkid to know pleasure?
He could wish for her to dive

into a surprising place—
neither the unwatered earth,
nor memory's ruinous hug,

but softness.

V.G.

MOM, RESURRECTED

Wear your coat. Wear your hat.
You'll get sick. Don't do that.
Call your mom. Call your mom.
A storm is coming. A storm.

Get some bread on the way home.
Get up. It's five minutes till. Hello?
I got you a delicious treat.
We'll be able to pay for heat.

That's for the holidays. Why did you open it.
What did you do this time. What did—
Just go away. Just beat it, all right?
Daddy and I waited all night.

How time flies. Time flies. Your fly's
open. Those kids,
they're a terrible influence.
Get a haircut. Your shirt is

unbuttoned. You make me pull out my hair.
Who do you think we are, millionaires?
Don't play hooky. Don't be MIA.
Don't slouch. ASAP. RIP. DOA.

Time to go tinkle. You've got
a frog in your throat. My God,
your cough: I don't like the way it sounds.
Lie down. Lie down. Lie down.

Don't say that while he is here.
It's five till. Up-up-up, my dear.
Why'd we splurge on that baby grand.
Be a man. Be like steel. Make a stand.

He'll be the death of me. The death.
Let me feel that forehead. Forehead.
Don't smoke. You'll ruin
your lungs. Don't be rude.

Don't catch a cold. It rained
all night. I know you drank.
I know you're drunk. Confess.
You're all alone now. Water the plants.

MOM, A LITURGY

It scares me that you're with a woman.
I am scared that you'll lose your job,
since, back in Russia, you would.
And because you are so young.

Actually, because you're not that young
anymore and should know better. I'm scared
that I can't help you, even my name's spelled
wrong in this alphabet.

Life continues, though. That calm boy:
I'm scared that he is not Russian.
Me, be less nervous? You're kidding.
You are my baby; I worry.

Scared, for piano and orchestra,
performed heavily, heavenly, Beethovenly,
and, when I can't bear it, scared deaf.
A zero-altitude flight over the keyboard.

How glorious that he's a Yank!
Sing: they don't cheat as much.
Sing: you'll clean when his mother visits.
Sing: you guys won't live like piglets.

I am so happy today, happy for you.
When Danny entered our lives,
we just knew. He waltzed in so musically,
and he hasn't ruined things, yet.

I know that you are with a woman.
I'm scared that you haven't left him.
It's so hard not to know what to tell you.
Surely he must be jealous.

Don't tell me fairy tales.
And if he thinks it is beautiful
that you and she are together,
then his love lacks fear,

and I'm afraid that's not love.
Listen to this pretty piece.

You say you all love each other,
then mention she wants to leave.

Why do you get so attached
when it bruises and scrapes you,
and I feel it all here? I don't need
your language, any language, to know.

"Scared" is not what I am, honey.
"Scarred" is more like it.
And, you say, sacred,
for some reason, to you.

V.G.

* * *

A bird builds up to a whole
then suddenly full she flies
her wings drafting figures
precisely on the sky

the clouds' mute light-lumps
the upwardly moving heat
a body of close clarity
passes over me

in the tender trust-full air
from its egg-blue workshop
feathers were molded into a bird
and draw my gaze upward.

THOREAU IN RUSSIA

Outside Moscow, a sixteen-year-old girl in thick glasses
looks for something in the littered, self-shedding woods.
At home the TV has exploded: Americans have brought down
their own skyscrapers, now they're destroying our ancient
homes, poisoning minds, snatching kids. The girl runs away,
reads Genri Toro, and a portable Walden rolls out.

By the hand, by her pinkie finger, Toro takes her away
from near the cranberry bush that almost shades shards
of vodka bottles, to the vaguely clean willow, *eva* in Russian,
not weeping, but bathing her lithe arms in the pond.
Genri liked washing off his nights, he announces:
Morning baths in the pond were my religious exercises,

and the best. The girl dips a toe: icy, October, black water.
Moscow's fall has been mute for boys and girls
noiselessly reading poems, microscopic, untranslated.
Do Americans read Genri? She forces herself to undress,
falls nude into the pond: a blast of liquid icicles, then
warmth. This, too, is real. It fits her like glasses.

As she hides in her jacket, she watches the oaks and maples
lift their yellow leaves—clubs, spades—against the sky's
booming blue gouache. It's just a bet, a quick card game,
yet the post-empire plants stand up, small-tall, no defenses.
Propped by a birch stump, Thoreau sits quietly with the girl:
irrelevant to their countries, legible to themselves.

MILK MUSHROOMS

For J.S.

Woodland sculptures, *Lactifluus piperatus*:
milk-flowing, milk-caps. Morning rolls
     over their generous white crowns,
          leaks down their
               dwindling
               columns,

                    wakes them up, and they babble:
                    Don't worry, darling, we are the safe
                    mushrooms, you've known us
                    since childhood: we are so happy
                    you've found us
                    here in the US—
                    kneel, please,
                    eat like Alice—

I pluck and bite. The mushroom bites me back—
capsaicin on the lips. "Edible but too bitter
to bother," *The Audubon Guide to Mushrooms*
declares. Then, memory on the lips: of famine, war;
women run home from work across a field,
quick-gathering buckets of these *gorkooshki—*
bitter littles—and salt them, boil, and cleanse
of sharpness. Hunger, poison, death itself—
they prayed—preventable—with salt and heat
and clean hands in the sink. And wasn't it?
Sad mushrooms, granting years of human life.
Milk mushrooms, granting years of *Soviet* life.
Cleansed from necessity, by the goddesses of—
necessity. While, living in my richest country, I
can't clean the world. Or heal my own mother
and father of their time—

Mushrooms of stinging milk. The best mushrooms
to grieve among. Their bare soft skins. My pets.
We sit and feel exactly what we feel.
No one will judge us as too-
anything: not here,
on this old
playground
of unwarm sun.

NO NEWS IS

"Hardly a man takes a half-hour's nap,"
grumbles Thoreau, "but when he wakes
he holds up his head and asks, 'What's the news?'"
O Thoreau, my adopted American uncle.
Per your instructions, I have impounded
Walden, harvested it, gorged myself on it,
and can now hike in Arkansas or Japan:
and—look!—a spruce, hung with periwinkle
sausages; by the ankles, a beige mushroom
that, picked freshly, lactates passionately
into my hand. I reach for my phone—I swear—
only to ask for the kind of news you would like:
"What are the names of these plants?"
Someone replies: *Weeping Norway spruce,*
Picea abies. Another names the mushroom:
Lactifluus. Uncle, I wish you could be with me
after the hike and see what I'm seeing
as I scroll down: one more birthday party
blown up by a drone, one more school
shooting here, out of twenty this year alone.
You said: "Knowing the principle,
one need not read memorable news,"
but this country has gone... memorable
since you've been gone. Ten walnut trees,
innocent, simple—just as you said—stand
around my cabin, comforting. They stand
like trees, knowing nothing of *Walden.*
No news is good news—only because
there is no news in the woods. Which is
where you stay, and where I leave you.

THANK YOU, AMERICA

For in you I can take Russian risks.
Like hunting mushrooms. In Moscow,
my passport marked me not as Real
Russian, but Jewish: smallish, dirtyish,
you-should-avoid-her-ish.
We had to hunt for our lives,
avoiding frivolities such as wild
mushrooms. My parents trapped
success in their respective arts. I
was a bit wild, too, at first,
spending my thirteenth year
trying to ensnare an achingly
curly-haired boy. The years came,
went, and I yearned to stop
hunting. *To collect*, instead—
so-beer-AHH-yum, we collect them—
mushrooms—in Russian.

U-S-A! U-S-A!—upside-down
toadstools are raining down on me,
that's how adorable it is to live
in this country. I've read guides
to mushrooms, forayed
with mycologists—most importantly,
realized no one was after me. And
I calmed down. Enough to feel
a *boletus bicolor* is about to debut
behind that oak, its pirouette still
unwitnessed, its leg, bestockinged
and yellow-red beneath a squishy,
full, burgundy tutu billowing, keeling over.
You see it—it's yours! No killing
required for collecting, or else the skillet:

butter bubbling, a little salt,
a ritual old as the world.

Dear U.S., I love your frontiersy
delusion—*anyone can learn*
not to die; of nature, at least.
You may not share my fearlessness
about the *fungus among us*: my own
Russian House dorm mates,
going on a foray, a.k.a. a barbecue,
brought sliced button mushrooms.
Right, mycophobes, try barbecuing *those.*
Still, you teach me how not to fear.
My American dream sleeps by my side
at night, our cat between us.
Collected like this, the nights, the days
are savory. You gave a *me*
that is collected, You. S., you,
and I am grateful. Thank you
for picking me.

V.G.

***

The snow must fly, the snow,
the bakery on the corner has to burn,
the child's mother will say, "Let's go!",
pull him away, and the wind has to blow,
and his feet in glossy boots must churn

gleaming slush. The pink maidens in chef's toques,
all decked out in lace, have to lift the crispness
of puff pastry delicacies with tongs,
and the child, who has a deep weakness
for his mother, dies in tears on the sidewalk,

and an old man who has to plod
home will tell you—oh God!—
how he loved stopping by here,
how he drank his coffee, his dear
dark coffee, his double shot:

"Only death," he whispers, "must be
bigger than this, only its reach
is stronger than this rustling, these scents..."—
and the thick, darkening fence
will solidify his voice and trust,

then, at last, the snow's heavy wing
will blanket and shield everything,
and the priest of knife-sharpening services
will do a wild dance in the haze
with a spark and a swing.

SOMETHING THERE IS THAT DOESN'T LOVE

...the ones like me. Something there is
that is repulsed by our sweatshirts,
pilled, our backpacks, full of bric-a-brac,
us, detained, on the floor, airport animals.
Something has claimed that my adopted
country's autobiography of openness
is finished. Something opens the mouths
of my Jewish family to mutter:
good for those terrorists to wait,
hope their turn doesn't come.
    So thank you to all
who sprang to protest when something
called all the ones like me criminals. Thank you
for translating your memory of Babcia,
of Abuelita, into this mother traveling home.
Your translation climbs over the walls,
helps us know each other. Gently
it joins our hands with Frost's, asking,
just one more time: why would anyone help?
And exactly what doesn't love a wall?

RUSSIAN 101

Родной [rod NOY]: native; my own;
darling; kindred soul (Russian)

Each word uttered in you is a chord.
Родной, you are helplessly plural,
these vocal cords do not just belong to my throat.
On the other side of the globe,
the sounds they utter could have caught
the multiple human sun.

That's the difference between a native language
and the set of expressions that newcomers grab.
Whatprice. Couldjews. Sincerely, your evil twin.
The otherling is brought home in a large plastic bag,
stirring a bit. We train it to use the litter box,
even if it remains a lynx.

But I'm not so faithful, either. It's been
fifteen years. I run from stilettoed lipstick,
avoid the Moscow Metro, ornate like the plague,
many-eyed with irritation and fatigue.
You can tell when I am drunk mostly
when I buy too many books.

But these tightly woven voices—bulging crowds
of foreigners and natives in Moscow—
behemoth jars of pickles my mother was paid with
in place of a salary—even those who feel betrayed
by what my parents did those fifteen years ago—
are loud within.

So hug me inside with your woe-voices,
hug me tightly with vice, родной.
The other part of you—
"darling," "kindred"—
sounds false, so allow me to reject that.

Deeper than kindred,
you are my stomach,
filled with a mute serenade.

V.G.

***

Do you know where that blue is from?
That sky-blue, the blue that was ground
by the Flemish apprentices in the future,
this cobalt, cerulean color?
Do you know where the sky is from,
why it is not guilty of any sin?
It's made out of one soul, then
another, and that doubly azure-blue
silence—
that's where Lazarus died twice.

TO RUSSIA, WITH YOU

1/ To the Epicenter

What transport takes flight to Russia for two women
who are in love? A bird of Aeroflot paradise? A quiet
Baltic Sea cruise? Slowdance with me on the deck,
you who wants to know the distant planet I'm from.
I'll pull my hand away when we arrive. Precaution,
not rejection. Let's run up the gray stone steps
of the Neva like friends; the blank for omitted *girl*
in *girlfriends* will be our breathing room. We'll wake
safe, in each other's arms, in a *babushka's* rental,
an Uzbek rug on the wall framing your pixie cut.

Let's walk to the farmers' market—it's here
every day of the week! Not the seasonal Thursdays
you're used to, those pale Jerusalem artichokes
grown near Boston or Madison. No: fists
of mauve peach flesh, sky-blue plummies,
and their tiny yellow sisters breathing warmths
of Azerbaijani into their Russian name: *ah–lyh–chah.*
Warm are the blue hawk tattoos on your arms.
Let me pull your t-shirt sleeves down,
now they almost cover up your birds.

I want to hear you moan as you dig
a slotted spoon into kloobneeka slowberries,
cherneeka sweetberries, forever-child-berries,
before-I-knew-berries, almost those berries
Tolstoy's Kitty preserved, and, listening to her
jam-making, Levin realized he wanted only
prose out of life. Will you wipe off an acidic
Antonovka apple for me? I dare you
to bite it, to smell beet greens dusted
by car exhaust, to know the toxic aroma

that keeps me awake on chilled sheets
in Non-Russia. In our imaginary invisible armor,
I kiss you on the lips and no one notices.
So prosaic. The drunks calling out "Best price!"
do not care, nor the lady with the perm,
the one cheating us a little on the scale,
nor her second cousin from Snake-o-grad,
nor a random nobody—I swear, they're not
walking over here, not pushing us apart—
Lesbianki! Who do they think they are, showing off!
Busy selling. They might not spit at us.

2 / No, Not to Russia

No time for sleeping tonight. Little son, Nathan-Natán,
wake up, let's fly to Odessa, where mommy was born,
where she spent her summers when she was a kid!
It's one of the worst times to go in Odessa's history,
but you are four, and will neither know nor care

about the war, nor about differences between the USSR,
Ukraine, and the Russian Federation. You will know
about three flights, yes, all on airplanes! Tiny cookies,
peanuts, endless cartoons. We will go to the beach
just like back then, yes, I once was little.

We will find mussel shells with the most mother-of-pearl,
and sit by the three-pane mirror in your great-grandfather's
apartment on Cosmonaut Street. I just learned
our family still owns that apartment. I'd thought
it was gone. I'd spent my childhood playing

with Grandma's Chinese baubles, green jewelry boxes,
little swans. Five minutes is all I want you to have.
Is the matchbox-shaped building ugly? I didn't think so.

But I need you to look at it and tell me it's gorgeous.
Chipped, mosaic-laden concrete balconies.

When one is little, it's joyful to walk under the first story.
I still love the intricate network of grapevines
clambering up them. Odessans continue to make wine
out of these grapes, but every week the terrorists
go for these balconies, for some reason. Killing

no one, we are told over tea. But why did you bring
Natánchik here, say the maybe-not-to-be-victims?
The conversation turns back to Brodsky, though faces
darken. Then we fly back to Connecticut. But would
I risk your life, kiddo, just to hear you say, *Mama,*

was that your home? I'd press my forehead against yours:
Now you know. Would I still feel that was home
when we got home? We live on Choice Street,
Hiding, Connecticut, where I can unbuckle you
and run-run-run with you to Wi-Fi and Facebook.

All the Odessans we know are still alive.

3 / To a Lake

Reader, how would you like to go to Lake Baikal?
I've heard it's on the other side of everything.

If you like fishing, we could fish for omul. It has
an unusual, delectable taste. I read all about that

in an e-mail. Or we could sit by a lakeside bonfire
in an Adirondack chair. (Check out the 31,000

Russian web search results for "Adirondack chair.")
I could help you look for a graying sunset

that hasn't murdered anyone, not yet.
Some ecologists stand, chatting, nearby.

Reader, aren't you and I speaking English?
Within minutes one ecologist, wearing

a hunting jacket, walks to us, pushes our chairs over
onto the sand, kicks us in the jaws, yells,

speek Rahshun, speek Rahshun. His beer-warm buddies
stand back, unsure of the right thing to do,

grinning just in case grinning is the right thing.
There is no mystery, none of that Russian soul

made up by Americans. Jews, openly gay people,
Ukrainians with an accent will suffer,

already do. No one should ever go to Russia.
In fact, Russians shouldn't go to Russia.

But this never happened. No one walked over,
no one screamed or hit us. The guys remain

by the bonfire in peace. We, closer to the lapping quiet.
Gritty warmth. The scent of dying dragonflies,

while some still flit about, fatly. Our home,
the world, dims into the sky's ornate auburn rug.

By this biggest and cleanest bowl of water
we are but an ordinary variant of the norm.

But a gray mass approaches. A swarm of mosquitoes
flying in from the lake? Or a mob coming?

Alychah plum yellow, the granulated jade
of the jewelry boxes on my grandmother's

makeup table, all swept off and replaced
by a dark gray—no, not gray, but the color you see

when you try to protect your face with your arms
and sweater. Something is coming at us

and this is all we've got. Help me, reader,
lift this gray like an outdated, grainy

satellite image of a country, help it bloom
into a mosaic, dappled like rivers

and horses and dogs, a thousand colors lush.

Olga Livshin is a Russian-American poet, translator, and essayist. She grew up in Odessa and Moscow before coming to San Diego as a teenager. Her work has been recognized by CALYX journal's Lois Cranston Memorial Prize and the Cambridge Sidewalk Poetry Project. Livshin's poems, translations, and essays are published in *The Kenyon Review, Poetry International,* and *Modern Poetry in Translation,* and her poems were translated into Persian by Mohsen Emadi. She holds a PhD in Slavic Languages and Literature and taught full-time at the university level before focusing on her poetry and translation. She lives outside Philadelphia, where she teaches creative writing and parents the poet Nathan Janco (seven years old at the date of publication).

Anna Akhmatova (1899-1966) was one of the most important Russian poets of the twentieth century and was twice nominated for the Nobel Prize. A prominent figure in the avant-garde of the 1910s and 1920s, the subject of much admiration and portraiture, she devoted much of her early poetry to the nuances of love relationships in her short, minimalistic poems. Her later poetry, such as *Requiem,* a long narrative poem about the imprisonment of her son in Stalin's labor camps, joins the lyric with the epic and the personal with the political. Akhmatova served as a model for many American feminist poets in the 1960s and 1970s.

Vladimir Gandelsman (b. 1948) is the 2011 recipient of Russia's highest award for poetry, the Moscow Reckoning. Born in Leningrad, he has lived near New York and St. Petersburg since 1991. He is the author of thirteen poetry collections, a verse novel and a collection of essays, and has received several prestigious awards in Russia. English translations of his work have appeared in *Modern Poetry in Translation, Notre Dame Review, The Common,* and *The Massachusetts Review.* He has also translated authors ranging from Shakespeare to Wallace Stevens, and Louise Glück to Dr. Seuss into Russian.

CPSIA information can be obtained
at www.ICGtesting.com
Printed in the USA
LVHW042103200323
742054LV00004B/642

9 780999 073735

"Olga Livshin has braided her own poems with her superb translations of Akhmatova and Gandelsman, poets she describes as 'ecstatic voices.' Livshin's voice, too, is ecstatic—and unflinching, and loving, and full of earned wisdom. In poem after poem, Livshin, who immigrated to the United States from Russia as a child, acknowledges the two Americas she knows firsthand: the one that fears and demonizes, and the one that welcomes. A *Life Replaced* is astonishingly beautiful, intelligent, and important."

—Maggie Smith

"What a blazing book! Fiery and original, its originality rooted partly in its passionate indebtedness. Olga Livshin has created her own genetic strands from the poems of Anna Akhmatova, Vladimir Gandelsman, and the Russian and English languages. Her passionate lyrics blend wit, sorrow, fury, mother love, and eros in lines at once tender, savage, and scarred by history."

—Rosanna Warren

"In this sensuous, funny, dark, and tender collection, Livshin documents her life as a Russian-American, American-Russian, an immigrant, a Jew, grappling with memory, home, exile, and survival amidst violent times, braided with the worlds of the interlocutors she translates. In reply to Anna Akhmatova, and to all of us, Livshin implores: 'This century is worse than those before it. Change something.'"

—Nomi Stone

"A true literary hybrid, a book-conversation in which Livshin's original poetry and her translations call to one another, blurring the borders between centuries, countries, and languages. Daring and tender, unapologetically political and deeply personal, it is a timely reminder of what it means to be an immigrant."

—Ellen Litman

ISBN 978-0-9990737-
51

9 780999 073735